Diesels

dragons & daffs

First published in Great Britain in 2009 by
Bryngold Books Ltd.,
Golden Oaks, 98 Brynau Wood, Cimla,
Neath, South Wales, SA11 3YQ.
www.bryngoldbooks.com

Typesetting, layout and design
by Bryngold Books

ISBN 978-1-905900-15-2

A ticket to nostalgia

From their earliest times there has always been a romanticism attached to our railways. Poets have waxed lyrical about them, artists have immortalised them on canvas while others have simply watched them thunder by. They have always had more to offer than simply nuts and bolts or whistles and bells as they carry people and parcels from place to place. Rationalisation, standardisation and even privatisation may well have combined to steal the cosy carriage compartments, opening windows or buffet car china. However, the colour, character and life that locomotives and trains add to both country and urban landscape while serving their daily duties have survived the gradual metamorphosis.

The images on the following pages prove that railways are as much a part of the scene as the seasons or the weather as they offer a ticket to travel on an unforgettable journey back in time to a distant diesel era. They were captured across South and West Wales when not only were the railways changing, but lots more in our lives too. Diesels, Dragons and Daffs is not a historical record, more a magical miscellany of images of the region's railways from the late 1970s to the early 1990s. The photographs show passenger, freight and line-side scenes in a way that railway buffs, regular passengers and those who simply watched the trains pass by, will enjoy for the shameless indulgence in nostalgia that it offers.

Thanks

 My sincere thanks are due to Stephen Miles for allowing me to use some of his wonderful images — those marked Photo: SKM are his — and to David Roberts for his vision and encouragement in creating this publication.

Dedication

This book is dedicated to the memory of my mother, who would have loved to have been around to see the result.

The author

 Colin Scott grew up in Bridgend and lived within sight and sound of the railway. It sparked an early interest and like every self-respecting young lad, he watched the trains at close quarters and collected the engine numbers. He witnessed the end of steam and the dawn of the diesel era. Better still, he later developed an interest in photography and so the two hobbies became linked. Colin has enjoyed a long career in local government working as a draughtsman, graphic designer, and surveyor. He has an embracing interest in all forms of transport, but that early love affair with railways lingers on. He is married with one son and lives in Neath. The delightful photographs in this book were taken with an artistic eye and truly capture the atmosphere of those distant diesel days across South Wales.

Trains serving the Rhymney Valley cosy up at the recently opened Cathays station, Cardiff, in July 1985.

Rooftop railway

A Rhymney to Penarth train approaches Bargoed in July 1991. The viaduct dwarfs the typical, stone-built South Wales valleys houses nestling below.

Sea side

A Milford Haven to Swansea train powers away from Ferryside on a bright and blue sky spring day in March 1982.

Underneath the arches

A Class 37 locomotive sweeps around the curve at Undy, Gwent, hauling a short west-bound steel train in April 1989.

Rail revival

Framed in foliage at Llangynwyd, a two car Pacer train makes its way from Bridgend to Maesteg on September 28, 1992. It marked the return of passenger services to the Llynfi Valley after an absence of more than two decades.

Druid delight

Looking more like a pair of Hornby models straight from the box, these Class 50 locomotives, seen at Pontyrhyl, visited the Garw Valley line in April 1992, hauling The Hoovering Druid enthusiasts special.

In February 1975 a Class 37 locomotive provides the motive power as a repaired NCB Austerity steam engine makes its return to Garw Colliery, Blaengarw. Photo: SKM

Oriental spice

The scenic splendour of the long climb up the Sugar Loaf mountain from Llandovery, surrounds a pair of Class 33 locomotives as they haul The Orient Express luxury Pullman train along the Heart of Wales line in March 1985. Photo: SKM

Shunters Kidwelly and Ashburnham at Llanelli station in January 1986. They were fitted with cut-down cabs to cope with restricted overhead clearance on the nearby Cwmmawr branch line. Photo: SKM

The Rhymney Valley complete with ribbons of traditional Welsh terraces envelopes a Sprinter train as it rolls down from Brithdir on its way to Penarth in July 1991.

All aboard

The signal is off for a Swansea-bound multiple unit at Ferryside, Carmarthenshire, in September 1987.

Spring cleaning

A slice of yellow punctuates the greenery as this permanent way train carrying recovered rails from Ebbw Vale runs down to Gaer Junction, Newport, in May 1987.

Marching on

Beautiful autumn colours surround
a Cardiff to Crewe train, leaving
Abergavenny and heading for the
Welsh Marches in October 1984.

Coastal corner

A Swansea to Pembroke Dock multiple unit approaches Ferryside in March 1982. The railway's route westward to Carmarthen provides passengers with some splendid coastal and estuary views.

The scene at Landore locomotive depot, Swansea, when on September 21, 1985, it was opened to visitors as part of celebrations to mark the 150th anniversary of the Great Western Railway.

Work & play

Welsh workhorse class 37 191 heads a rugby special through Margam in March 1978. The loco was new to Landore in February 1964 as D6891. Photo: SKM

Power rangers

A pair of Class 37 locomotives provide power for the Glamorgan Growler rail tour of May 6, 1989. With only sheep for company, the special approaches Cwmbargoed, at the top of the remote Taff-Bargoed valley, after a six mile climb from Nelson. Photo: SKM

Highs & lows

Viewed from Old Castle Down, a London-bound High Speed Train slices its way through deep limestone cuttings at Ewenny, in February 1991. The train had been diverted along the scenic Vale of Glamorgan line because of engineering work.

The 16.30 train from Milford Haven to Swansea is caught in the late afternoon sun at Ferryside during June 1985.

Early warning

This period BR(W) enamel sign and crossing gates remained at Rhymney in 1981. A reminder of a bygone era.

Patriotic perspective

A late showing of daffodils in May 1988 complements a smartly turned out Class 37 locomotive as it descends Stormy Bank near Pyle with empty hopper wagons.

Hearty starter

Weak sunshine greets the morning Swansea to Shrewsbury service, as it crosses the River Loughor at Pontarddulais in November 1983.

Sharp end

Still and silent this HST locomotive shows off its new coat of paint and its high speed aerodynamics, in September 1991.

Snow white

A Valley Lines Sprinter struggles away from Radyr with a service to Treherbert during the snowy weather of January 31, 1991.

Merry-go-round

A grey Class 37 locomotive arrives at Aberthaw with a 'merry-go-round' train of coal for the power station in October 1988.

Hide and seek

Cut-down shunter 08 995 Kidwelly, in Coal Sector livery, at rest at the back of Landore depot, Swansea in April 1991.

A Western class hydraulic locomotive speeds through Burry Port with a Paddington to Tenby express on a summer Saturday in August 1971. Photo: SKM

Buckets and spades

A Valley Lines diesel multiple unit arrives at Barry Island station on a warm summer afternoon in 1984. The traditional railway architecture was still much in evidence there at the time.

Happy New Year

Cardiff Canton diesel depot plays host to a variety of locomotives in their different liveries at rest on New Year's Day, 1989.

Going green
Swansea Burrows' resident shunter 08 896 heads through the undergrowth in August 1991, having taken a rake of coal containers to the quayside at nearby King's Dock.

Red used to mean only one thing on the railway — danger. Things were different by 1991, as these regimental rows of canopy pillars at Newport station show.

Stormy struggle

Around 3,000 tons of iron ore from Port Talbot tidal harbour terminal, are being dragged up to Pyle by two Class 37 locomotives bound for Llanwern Steelworks, Newport in July 1991.

Smoke signals

A snow covered Mynydd Ty-Isaf makes an imposing backdrop as a DMU in the short-lived white and blue livery leaves Treherbert with a trail of smoke behind it in January 1978. Photo: SKM

Work done for the day, the driver of this class 56 locomotive makes his way to clock off at Canton diesel depot, Cardiff, in the summer of 1990.

The daffodils at Newport station dance in the breeze as Class 37 locomotive 711 Tremorfa Steelworks in colourful Trainload Metals sector livery passes through in March 1990 .

Journey's end

Flagship Class 47 locomotive Great Western, crawls to the breakwater over a line unused for many years, after hauling The Orient Express to Fishguard as part of the GWR's 150 year salute in 1985.

Early bird

A Cardiff to Swansea HST climbs away from Neath early on a misty morning in April 1987. The leading power car has been repainted in the latest version of InterCity livery.

Silent night

Eight Class 37 locomotives cosset a solitary Class 08 at Godfrey Road stabling point, Newport, during an autumn evening in 1988.

Bush baby

Summer Sunday engineering works in 1979 brought this Swansea to Paddington service bursting through the trees at Penyfai, near Bridgend.

Sunset sweep

Back-lit by the evening sun, a High Speed Train assumes a magical appearance as it heads west through Magor in April 1989.

Mellow yellow

A Class 33 locomotive waits at Cardiff Central station's Platform 2 with a Crewe bound train in April 1984.

Capital cargo

The area around Pengam Freightliner terminal in Cardiff was once a hive of activity, as this trio of Class 37s, seen in July 1991, with a backdrop of cargo containers demonstrates.

Two Class 20 locomotives brought a rail tour to the Dulais Valley on July 28, 1991. Here the visitors are seen climbing past the site of the former Dilwyn colliery near Seven Sisters, silhouetted against a conifer plantation.

Tywi traveller

A Swansea-bound
diesel multiple unit briefly
disturbs the tranquility of a
summer's afternoon as it
slices between the rolling
Carmarthenshire hills and the
waters of the Tywi estuary
near Ferryside in June 1985.

Valley viewpoint

A rail tour approaches Neath & Brecon junction at Neath after visiting the Vale of Neath and Dulais Valley branches in October 1993.

Rooftop rainbow
A patchwork of multi-coloured rooftops surrounds a multiple unit at Pontypridd in April 1988.

Sunday service

Punctuating the greenery surrounding Neath & Brecon Junction at Neath, Network SouthEast liveried locomotive 47 709 was in charge of a Swansea to Paddington Sunday service in April 1991.

At Cwm Mawr in June 1979, a trio of cut-down Class 03 locomotives prepare to take an afternoon train of hoppers to Burry Port. On the right is a privately owned former Class 07 shunter. Photo: SKM

CLASS 35. 37. 47. 52 ENGINES PROHIBITED BEYOND THIS POINT

7500

Far flung

Locomotive 47 500 dares not move an inch further at Fishguard Harbour! The sign had weathered well, considering the Class 35s (Hymeks) and the Class 52s (Westerns) it referred to had gone many years earlier.

Signals and snow

The 12.22 Cardiff Central to Radyr train approaches its destination on January 31, 1991, framed by signal gantries. The reds and yellows make a glorious statement against the winter white-out.

Dragon's den

A spotless 47 616 proudly displays its bilingual nameplate at the former Riverside station at Cardiff Central, after its naming ceremony on July 6, 1985.

A Brush Type 4 Class 47 locomotive arrives at Severn Tunnel Junction with a company train carrying Ford cars from Dagenham in March 1973. The former steam shed here had been put to use as a car distribution centre. Photo: SKM

A train of empty mineral wagons hauled by a Class 37 locomotive passes King's Dock junction, Swansea Docks, late on a June evening in 1975 on its way to Pantyffynon, Ammanford. Photo: SKM

Chocolate time

Along with many commemorative events held to mark the 150th anniversary of the Great Western Railway, this train, seen in Swansea in May 1986, was painted in the GWR chocolate and cream livery.

Sunday service

Locomotive 47 716 Duke of Edinburgh's Award swoops down Skewen Bank with a Sunday evening Paddington service in September 1990.

Royal box

The weathered roof of Ferryside signal box frames a Milford Haven to Swansea local train, hauled by 47 620 Windsor Castle during September 1985.

A Valley Lines multiple unit waits at Treherbert in the summer of 1984.
The deserted sidings suggest it was a busy time of day further south.

Oil aboard

Locomotive 56 035 Taff Merthyr skirts the coast at Ferryside, returning empty oil tanks to one of the Milford Haven refineries in September 1987.

The 1990s transitional period in BR's history is typified by this multi-liveried parcels train at Briton Ferry in May 1991. The loco in charge is the unique Provincial-liveried 47 475.

Express delivery

The South Wales Pullman approaches journeys end at Swansea after its express run from Paddington, in December 1971. The train was the forerunner of the familiar High Speed Trains that became common place in later years. Photo: SKM

Weedy worker

Taunted by an array of line-side blooms this weedkiller train, hauled by a privately owned Class 20 locomotive, does its annual duty at Neath Abbey on April 19, 1989.

Job seeker

Hurrying to its next job, a drab Class 37 locomotive adds to the greyness of an autumn day as it crosses the River Ogmore at Wildmill, Bridgend in October 1987.

Snow patrol
The still, icy waters of the River Neath at low tide reflect a multiple unit heading out of Neath in January 1985.

The paintwork of brand new locomotive 60 062 Samuel Johnson gleams in the afternoon sun, as it passes BP Llandarcy with its train of grubby tankers, in July 1991.

Wagon train

A class 60 locomotive passes Llangewydd Court Farm after snaking its way over Stormy Down with it's train of ore wagons during the autumn of 1995.

All in a days work

In April 1977 one of the Swansea Docks shunters propels a train of steel coil into the main departure sidings at King's Dock Junction. Now only a single line remains to serve King's Dock low level from **Burrows Yard.** Photo: SKM

Era's end

The very last coal from the Llynfi Valley was recovered from the stockpiled remains at St John's Colliery, Maesteg, on February 23, 1993. Locomotive 37 796 waits patiently at the colliery's waterlogged loading pad to make the final journey.

Cutting edge

A pair of Class 33 locomotives hauling an enthusiasts special to Carmarthen slice through the deep cutting as they head into Peniel Green tunnel on the Swansea District Line, May 1988.

Newly painted in Trainload Coal Sector livery and appropriately named The Coal Merchants' Association of Scotland, locomotive 37 235 hauls a Bristol-bound train of household coal through Severn Tunnel Junction, in April 1989.

Winter wonderland

Snow and ice caused widespread disruption to services on January 8,1985, but this DMU seen through a wintry landscape at Skewen was a welcome sight as it operated a hastily arranged relief service to Swansea.

Up the junction

Newly refurbished locomotive 37 428 David Lloyd George with a train of coal empties at Gaer Junction, Newport, during May 1987.

The Parcels Sector adopted a bright red livery to complement Royal Mail, its principle customer. Several redundant DMUs were modified to carry parcels, including this set brightening up Cardiff Riverside in June 1990.

Grave matters

Their days of thundering along the main line well and truly over, by June 1978 the remains of these Western diesel hydraulics serve as a poignant reminder of the glory days of the early diesel era.